D1219226

ECOLOGY WATCH

POLAR LANDS

Rodney Aldis

DILLON PRESS
NEW YORK

First American publication 1992 by Dillon Press, Macmillan Publishing Company, 866 Third Avenue, New York, NY 10022

Macmillan Publishing Company is part of the Maxwell Communication Group of Companies

First published by Evans Brothers Limited, 2A Portman Mansions, Chiltern Street, London W1M 1LE

Typeset in England by Fleetlines Typesetters, Southend-on-Sea
Printed in Spain by GRAFO, S.A.—Bilbao

10 9 8 7 6 5 4 3 2 1

Aldis, Rodney.
    Polar lands / Rodney Aldis.
        p. cm.— (Ecology watch)
    Includes index.
    Summary: Discusses plant and animal life at the poles and the way climate and ecology affect that life.
    ISBN 0-87518-494-4
    1. Ecology—Polar regions—Juvenile literature. 2. Polar regions—Juvenile literature. [1. Polar regions. 2. Ecology—Polar regions.] I. Title. II. Series.
QH541.5.P6A43 1992
574.5'262—dc20   91-34170

Acknowledgments

Editor: Su Swallow
Design: Neil Sayer
Production: Jenny Mulvanny

Illustrations: David Gardner, Graeme Chambers
Maps: Hardlines, Charlbury

For permission to reproduce copyright material the author and publishers gratefully acknowledge the following:

Cover (Inuit in hunting kayak, Greenland) John Lythgoe, Planet Earth Pictures
Title page (Harp seal pup) J M Terhune/Biofotos

p4 Rick Price, Survival Anglia **p5** Wedigo Ferchland, Bruce Coleman Limited **p6** B & C Alexander **p7** Norbert Rosing, Bruce Coleman Limited **p8** Francisco J Erize, Bruce Coleman Limited **p9** B & C Alexander **p10**(left) B & C Alexander, (right) Wendy Else, B & C Alexander **p11** Stephen J Krasemann, Bruce Coleman Limited **p12** Soames Summerhays/Biofotos **p13** (top) B & C Calhoun, Bruce Coleman Limited, (bottom) Steve Kaufman, Bruce Coleman Limited **p14** Dr Eckart Pott, Bruce Coleman Limited **p15** Heather Angel **p16** Derek Fordham, Arctic Camera, **p17** (inset) B & C Alexander, (top) Heather Angel, (bottom) Bruce Coleman Limited **p18** (top) B & C Alexander, (bottom) B & C Alexander, Bruce Coleman Limited **p19** B & C Alexander **p20** James D Watt, Planet Earth Pictures **p21** B & C Alexander, (inset) ECOSCENE/Farmar **p22** (left) Steven C Kaufman, Bruce Coleman Limited. (right) B & C Alexander **p23** Dr Eckart Pott, Bruce Coleman Limited **p24** ECOSCENE/Farmar **p25** (top) Paul Meitz, Bruce Coleman Limited. (bottom) B & C Alexander **p26** David A Ponton, Planet Earth Pictures, (inset) Joel Bennett, Survival Anglia **p27** Erwin & Peggy Bauer, Bruce Coleman Limited **p28** (top) ECOSCENE/Cooper, (bottom) Kenneth W Fink, Ardea London Ltd **p29** Abbotts Packaging Ltd, Bruce Coleman Limited **p30** B & C Alexander **p32** B & C Alexander **p33** B & C Alexander **p34** Heather Angel **p35** (left) B & C Alexander, (right) Norbert Rosing, Bruce Coleman Limited **p36** (left) Wayne Lankinen, Bruce Coleman Limited (right), Francisco Erize, Bruce Coleman Limited **p37** Hans Reinhard, Bruce Coleman Limited **p38** John Shaw, Bruce Coleman Limited **p39** (top) B & C Alexander, (bottom) Leonard Lee Rue III, Bruce Coleman Limited **p40** Mike Tracey, Survival Anglia **p43** Bryn Campbell, Biofotos **p44** Soames Summerhays/Biofotos

Contents

Introduction

The Earth has two polar regions. The land and seas around the North Pole are known as the Arctic. At the other end of the Earth, around the South Pole, lies Antarctica.

Until the nineteenth century the Antarctic had never been visited by humans. The animals there had never had any reason to evolve ways of protecting themselves against hunters, so it was easy for people to kill whales and seals in huge numbers. But as the animal populations fell, hunting became unprofitable and the slaughter stopped. Today Antarctic wildlife is well protected against overhunting and, for the moment at least, the continent is dedicated to scientific research.

The Arctic has had a very different history. As the ice sheets melted at the end of the last ice age, people were able to move farther and farther north, following the rivers and coasts exposed by the retreating ice. Northern Scandinavia was the first part of the Arctic to be colonized: the first people arrived soon after the land was free of the ice sheets, about 8,000 years ago.

To the east, the **tundras** and coasts of the Russian Arctic were settled by 20 or so different tribes. The ancestors of the **Inuit** crossed into North America about 6,000 years ago from Siberia and spread along the coasts of Arctic Canada and Greenland. The settlers learned to live in balance with the Arctic land and seas, taking what they needed in order to live, but no more. Their kill of whales, seals, bears, and caribou was never enough to endanger the species on which they depended.

When the Europeans arrived in the Arctic,

▽ Penguins live in Antarctica, but not in the Arctic.

△ People have lived in the Arctic for thousands of years. In Greenland, fishing is the most important industry.

they hunted whales, seals, and polar bears for profit. Today, although there are still worries about overfishing in the Arctic seas, hunting is generally well controlled. But the Arctic is under threat from a different direction. The oil and minerals are more valuable than whale blubber or polar skins ever were, and finding and then exploiting these resources can damage the Arctic habitats. There is also always the risk of an oil spill, a particular problem in these fragile habitats, which take a long time to recover because of the cold climate. The **indigenous people** of the Arctic are also affected by the new industries as outsiders move in to work, bringing with them different cultures and ways of life.

Another threat concerns not just the polar regions but the whole world. If carbon dioxide and other **greenhouse gases** cause the world's climate to become warmer, the massive **ice caps** in Antarctica and Greenland may melt. This would raise the level of the oceans and lead to widespread flooding of cities and farming areas.

An understanding of the polar regions is necessary not only to protect the polar people and the polar wildlife but probably also to help protect the rest of the planet.

Words printed in **bold** are explained at the end of each section.

tundra—a vast treeless area of land in the Arctic.
Inuit—Eskimos.
indigenous people—people who are native to a country or region.
greenhouse gases—gases such as carbon dioxide that trap heat in the atmosphere.
ice caps—thick masses of ice and snow that permanently cover an area of land.

Close-up on climate

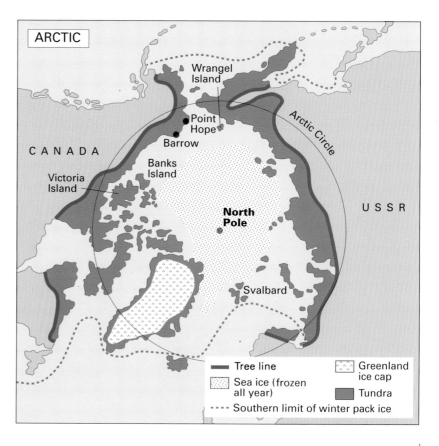

A special feature of the polar summer is the continuous daylight, which allows plants on land and in the sea to grow almost continuously for several weeks of the year. At the North Pole the sun rises on March 21 and does not set again until September 22. And once it has set, it does not rise again until the following March, which means there is no real daylight during the winter. At the South Pole the pattern is the same, except that summer and winter are at the opposite times of year. The polar regions, therefore, get their yearly quota of daylight and darkness mostly in two large servings.

Circles around the Poles

The imaginary lines we call the Arctic and Antarctic Circles do not mark accurately the

▽ As one approaches the tundra in the Arctic, the trees gradually peter out.

boundaries of the polar regions, for these lines are not related to major changes in types of plants and animals. For example, in Norway, trees grow far north of the Arctic Circle whereas in eastern Canada they stop growing a long way south of it.

Geographers prefer to define the Arctic by climate rather than by the less precise forest-tundra boundary. Officially the boundary is an imaginary line on the Earth's surface

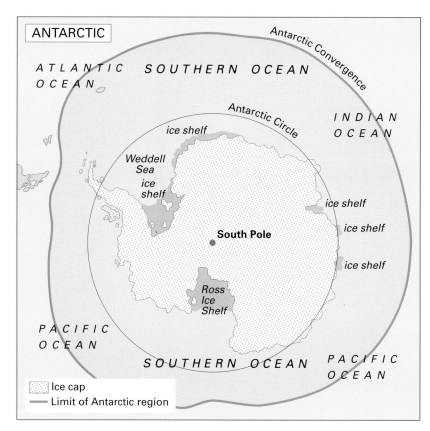

ANTARCTIC

ATLANTIC OCEAN

SOUTHERN OCEAN

Antarctic Convergence

Antarctic Circle

INDIAN OCEAN

ice shelf

Weddell Sea ice shelf

ice shelf

South Pole

ice shelf

ice shelf

PACIFIC OCEAN

Ross Ice Shelf

SOUTHERN OCEAN

PACIFIC OCEAN

Ice cap
Limit of Antarctic region

△ Curtains of colored light, called the aurora borealis or northern lights, sometimes fill the Arctic sky. The same effect also occurs in the Antarctic.

linking the points where the average temperature for the warmest month is 50°F. Such a line is called an isotherm. However, trees need at least one summer month with a temperature of at least 50°F, so the climatic boundary more or less follows the northern limit of the forests. (But differences in soils and exposure to winds from place to place means the 50°F isotherm for July does not fit exactly with the northern forest boundary.)

The boundary of the Antarctic is out on the open ocean and is where the cold north-flowing waters of the Antarctic Ocean converge (meet) with warm water flowing south from the tropics (see map). Cold and hot water do not mix easily, so the polar water does not mix easily with the tropical water. The colder, denser Antarctic water sinks beneath the warmer, less dense tropical water. The convergence of Antarctic and tropical water cannot be seen in the color of the water, but the tropical water is saltier. The convergence marks a change in the environment as great as that between the treeless tundra and the coniferous forests in the northern hemisphere, for the two types of water have different types of marine plants and animals.

Cold and dry
Surprisingly perhaps, the air in polar regions is quite dry. This is because cold air cannot hold very much water vapor—but the humidity can be high. Areas of open water that occur here and there amid the sea ice can be spotted by the "smoke" that hangs over the open water. The smoke is really fog that forms as the water vapor condenses.
Precipitation of all types—snow, rain, fog, and dew—is low, and over large parts of the tundra the plants suffer from water shortage as much as they do in warm deserts. This is why the really dry parts of the tundra, such as those on the islands in the Canadian High Arctic, are a polar desert.

Poles apart
The Antarctic polar region has at its center a permanently ice-covered continent surrounded by an ocean. The Arctic is a permanently ice-covered ocean almost enclosed by land. These differences make the climate in the Antarctic more severe than in the Arctic because land loses (and gains) heat faster than oceans do.

However, the coldness of Antarctica is increased because at its center the

◁ In winter in the Antarctic, the sea freezes so quickly that the ice spreads out at a rate of more than 2.5 miles per day. At its greatest extent, the sea ice more than doubles the area of the Antarctic ice.

▷ When the snow melts in the Arctic tundra, the permafrost below the surface keeps water from soaking into the soil. Some plants thrive in the boggy ground, and millions of birds feed and breed here.

mountains are very high. It is, in fact, the continent with the highest average altitude. Half of the continent is more than 10,000 feet above sea level. As a result of its height, some 99 percent of the continent is covered by an ice sheet. The snow and ice, being white, reflect most of the sun's rays. Very few of the sun's rays are converted into heat, so the air above the ice is not warmed. Cold air, which is heavier than warm air, also drains off the continent and spreads over the ocean. This cold air makes the southern hemisphere several degrees colder than the northern hemisphere.

Antarctica once had a much warmer climate, but the rich variety of subtropical plants and reptiles that lived there became extinct as the climate worsened and the massive ice sheet grew. Because Antarctica is isolated from other continents by many miles of ocean, the only living things that can reach it are those that can swim, fly, float in the sea or air, or be carried there by other living things. So, unlike the Arctic, Antarctica has very few kinds of advanced plants, and no true land-living mammals, such as caribou and lemmings. However, the difference in the marine life of the two regions is much less (see page 20).

Ice, ice almost everywhere

Ice is never far away in the polar regions. It is found above ground and beneath it, and on the surface of the seas. It has shaped—and still is shaping—the land, and for some animals, such as polar bears and seals, it is an important part of their habitat.

The permanent ice of glaciers and inland ice sheets is the most extreme polar habitat. Permanent ice accumulates wherever more snow falls in the winter than melts during the summer. Most of the Antarctic continent and Greenland are covered by ice sheets, and together they hold about 75 percent of the earth's fresh water.

In the Arctic, most of the tundra is frozen to depths of up to 2,625 feet. Only the top 6 to 10 feet melt in the short summers. The frozen ground is called permafrost, and it too is an important feature of the landscape for wildlife. Although the precipitation is low, there is plenty of surface water over much of the tundra during the summer because the permafrost keeps water from seeping into the soil. The wet ground is the habitat for plants such as sedges and cotton grass (see page 30), and these plants are food for waterfowl. The tundra bogs are also the breeding grounds of many wading birds that visit the Arctic in the summer.

△ Ice makes different patterns as the sea freezes. Frost flowers form round salt crystals as the sea water begins to freeze.

▷ Pancake ice forms later in the freezing process.

What kind of ice?

Ice is also a major feature of the polar oceans. There are three kinds of ice on the polar seas: icebergs, pack ice, and landfast ice. Each plays its part in the environment and affects the wildlife in the area.

Wherever glaciers and ice sheets reach the coast, large hunks of ice break away into the sea and drift with the currents, sometimes drifting for many miles before they completely melt. The average iceberg is about the size of a shopping mall, and some are much larger. Some sea birds use icebergs as resting platforms (see page 40). If icebergs become grounded in bays and fiords they add fresh water to the sea (see page 12).

Most of the ice in the polar oceans is formed not from snow but by the freezing of the surface water of the sea in the winter. The frozen seawater makes up the pack ice, which is a major feature of both the Arctic and the Antarctic oceans. The central part of the Arctic Ocean is permanently frozen, but around this core there is an area where higher summer temperatures and ocean currents break up the pack ice in the summer. In the Antarctic the winter pack ice may stretch out to the **convergence zone**, but here too a combination of warmer temperatures in summer and strong currents breaks up the ice into sheets of floating ice called floes. The floes are swept around the continent in a counterclockwise direction, and pile up as an ice barrier around the continent. Ships sailing to the Antarctic have to find a way through this ring of ice.

Landfast ice—that is, sea ice attached to the land—develops in early winter as the temperatures drop. In midwinter the landfast ice makes a link between the land and the offshore pack ice. In the spring, however, the pack ice breaks up before the landfast ice melts, and for a few weeks in the spring and early summer the landfast ice forms a wide shelf that separates the shore from the open water. It is along the edge of the landfast ice in the Arctic that polar bears and Inuit hunters search for seals at this time of year.

Wildlife on—and under—the ice

Very little light can penetrate thick ice. The central part of the Arctic Ocean is very poor in plant and animal life, although winter sea ice is important for some types of algae that spend the winter attached to its undersurface. When the ice breaks up in spring, the "grass of the oceans" thrives in the sunlight falling on the water.

In some places the seas are kept free of ice by wind and currents, even in the winter. These areas of open water are called polynyas, and they are extremely important to wildlife, especially whales, seals, polar bears, and sea birds. Because of the richness of the wildlife, polynyas are also important hunting and fishing areas for the Inuit. There is a polynya located in the eastern Canadian Arctic, near Baffin Island, which is used for part of the year by large numbers of North American birds, as well as by many narwhal and beluga whales.

▽ A harp seal comes up for air between ice floes.

Other rich areas for wildlife are where Arctic waters flow southward into seas that are ice-free during the summer. Where the nutrient-rich polar waters reach the sunlight in ice-free areas, conditions are ideal for polar wildlife. The sea between Greenland and Svalbard (a group of islands; see map on page 6), for example, is incredibly rich in plankton, fish, whales, seals, and sea birds.

In the Antarctic Ocean most of the pack ice melts in the summer and the seas are full of plankton, fish, sea birds, and seals. Whales were also abundant until their numbers were reduced by hunting.

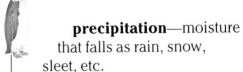

precipitation—moisture that falls as rain, snow, sleet, etc.
convergence zone—(here) the place where the cold Antarctic waters meet the warm tropical waters.

11

Polar plants

In the sea

An important feature of the polar regions is that the seas are rich in nutrients, while the land is poor. The cold polar water is rich in phosphates, nitrates, and other minerals that plants need, as well as having more dissolved carbon dioxide and oxygen gases than warmer water. It is only sunlight that is needed to bring life to this rich cocktail of nutrients, and wherever the ocean is free of sea ice there is plenty of sunshine for several weeks around midsummer.

In the seas the most important plants are the small ones that make up the plant plankton. The plant plankton traps sunlight energy and uses it to make food from the nutrients dissolved in the sea water. However, in the sea, as on the land, a plant or animal usually ends up being food for something else. The plant plankton is just the beginning of a food chain in which animals in each stage of the chain eat the living things in the stage beneath them.

The animal plankton eats the plant plankton, and is itself eaten by small fish, which are eaten by larger fish and squid. The larger fish are eaten in turn by whales, seals, and sea birds. At the top of the chain are polar bears and humans. Some animals are part of food chains on land and in the sea.

Melting ice

Pack ice loses much of its salt as it gets older. In the spring, water from melting pack ice, and also to some extent from icebergs (shown here), forms a layer of lighter, fresher water that sits above the saltier, heavier water beneath. Nutrients are trapped in this layer and the plant plankton thrives. Plankton "blooms" follow the retreating ice edge in spring and summer.

△ Saxifrage   ▷ Tundra shrubs

On the land

The polar regions are harsh environments for land plants. The summers are short and mostly cool, and because it is too cold for many trees to grow, there are no forests to slow the speed of cold winds. The dry climate means that plants can suffer from a lack of moisture almost as much as those in a desert, especially when strong winds increase the evaporation of water from their leaves. Then there is the problem of the freezing and thawing of the soil, which churns the soil particles. This movement makes it difficult for plants to keep their roots in one place and undamaged.

The solution to these problems is to keep low. A rock, even a stone, can produce a small pocket of still air several degrees warmer than exposed areas a little more than an inch away. There is, therefore, a great advantage in being short, since this allows a plant to take advantage of even a small sheltered place.

It also helps to be compact. Hollows in the ground are not only more sheltered, but they also fill with snow. Snow acts as a blanket through the worst of the weather and in spring and summer provides plants with a plentiful supply of water for several weeks— a natural irrigation supply in a cold desert. However, the weight of snow can damage leaves and stems. Many of the Arctic plants have shapes like cushions or grow as tussocks. This allows the plant to spread the weight of the snow, and it protects the center of the plant from wind.

The harsher the polar environment, the smaller and closer the plants are to the ground. Along the sheltered valleys of the southern Arctic, ribbons of forest extend into the tundra almost like tentacles expanding from the great belt of coniferous forest that lies to the south. However, the farther north we go the shorter trees—such as birch and willow—become, until they are no more than shrubs. In the far north they trail along the ground, and then only in the most sheltered places.

Too cold for comfort

The Antarctic continent is the more extreme of the two polar regions. So far only two species of "advanced" plants have been found there. All the others are simple plants such as algae, lichens, and mosses, which are able to tolerate severe weather.

Despite the harsh conditions it is amazing where plants are found. Even in the mountains of the Antarctic the snowfields are sometimes stained pink by a single-celled alga. It lives among the particles of snow, getting its energy from the sunlight and its nutrients from the snow. Another kind of alga manages, incredibly, to live between the minute cracks of hard rock.

On the surface of bare rocks and ground, however, we find more obvious plants—the lichens. They are plants formed by algae and fungi living together. Lichens come in many colors and forms. Some are flat, some are crusty, others are curly strips, and some look like hairs.

Lichens are often the first plants to colonize bare ground, and as they die and rot they help to form soils in which other plants such as mosses can thrive. In the Arctic, the mosses in turn speed up soil formation. As they die their leaves and stems enrich the soil, so that more advanced plants such as grasses are able to take root. These advanced plants are more restricted by where they can grow than the simpler plants, but it is the advanced plants that form the major food for the herbivores (plant-eating animals). The Arctic caribou, however, do rely on lichens, especially in the winter.

▷ Few plants, apart from lichens, grow in the Antarctic.

◁ In autumn, dwarf birch and willow trees fill the Arctic tundra with color, but the snow will soon return.

Plants for the animals

In the sheltered places the plants include mountain avens, saxifrages, moss campions, willowherbs, and crowfoots. Many of these plants hug the ground and some, such as the moss campions, grow in compact clumps. The bilberry, crowberry, bearberry and cloudberry often form a thick carpet of shrubby growth over sheltered ground and the drier parts of the tundra bogs. In late summer they produce energy-rich berries that attract many animals, including grizzly and black bears. The bears feed on the berries to fatten up just before they retire to their winter dens.

One of the most important plants for the herbivores is the arctic willow. Depending upon conditions such as wind and water supply, this woody plant may be found trailing along the ground or growing as a shrub up to three feet or more high. The leaves and buds of the willow are nutritious and are a major food for caribou, musk oxen, and ptarmigan.

Although many of the advanced arctic plants produce flowers, most of them do not rely upon seeds to grow new plants. The summers are just too short and unpredictable for most plants to flower and produce seeds, and there are few animals that can carry pollen from plant to plant. Instead, most plants reproduce from trailing stems or runners, which develop roots where they touch suitable areas of soil. In time the connecting stems are broken by animals or by wear and tear. This type of reproduction means that large parts of the tundra can be covered by a single species of plant.

Life among the plants

The plant communities of the Arctic tundra and freshwater lakes and rivers provide food and shelter for many small **invertebrates**. These invertebrates are extremely important as food for the great numbers of wading birds, ducks, and geese that are raised each year on the tundra, and also for the freshwater fishes – like trout, char, salmon, and arctic grayling.

Most of the invertebrates are various kinds

△ Bilberries and other autumn fruits are collected by people and animals in the Arctic.

of insects, spiders, mites, and snails. Compared with the warmer environments to the south, the number of invertebrate species is not very great. But this does not mean that the numbers of animals belonging to a particular species is low. Anyone who has visited the tundra of the southern Arctic in July will tell you that the air is alive with hordes of swarming and biting insects, including mosquitoes, midges, and blackflies. Butterflies and moths are also present, the adults pollinating the flowering plants. Plant-sucking insects are the most common types of insects, however, and include weevils, craneflies, and springtails.

Not all insects are pure plant feeders. Female mosquitoes, midges, and blackflies need the protein provided by a meal of bird or mammal blood before they can lay their eggs. These insects are able to detect warm-blooded animals sometimes a mile or two away by their body heat. In midsummer, biting and swarming insects harass animals such as caribou. The warble fly is also a parasite of caribou. The female lays its eggs in the caribou's coat and the maggots bore their way under the skin. Large numbers of warble flies can weaken the animal and make it more likely to be killed by wolves.

△ The arctic char (inset) feeds on small invertebrates in rivers and lakes.

Waiting out the winter

Most invertebrates survive the winter by burying themselves in the soil or, if they live in rivers and lakes, in the mud on the bottom. Very few of the adult insects survive into the winter. Instead, the eggs they laid in summer hatch into **larvae**, which can withstand the winter cold—often by producing various kinds of antifreeze, which keeps ice from forming inside their bodies.

Invertebrates are cold-blooded animals, so the temperature of their bodies is more or less the same as the temperature of the surrounding water or air. Many Arctic invertebrates have dark colors that help them to absorb heat much better than if they were light colored.

In Antarctica the variety of invertebrates is much less than in the Arctic. Species of springtails and mites that spend all or most of their time in the soil, and among the lichens and mosses just above the surface, are the most numerous invertebrates.

△ In the Arctic, many butterflies and other insects have dark colors to help them absorb heat from the sun.

invertebrates—animals without backbones.

larvae—the young stage of some insects, which is often very different from the adult stage.

17

Hunters of the wilderness

Although the Arctic tundra is rich in wild berries for a month or so each year, there are few plants on which humans can rely for food. So indigenous peoples have to hunt animals to obtain food. The most reliable supplies come from the seas and coasts, which support whales, seals, freshwater birds, sea birds, and fish. That is why most of the Inuit live near the coast and hunt marine mammals, although they also hunt caribou for part of the year.

The lives of the Inuit are bound closely to the animals they hunt. Because humans are at the top of the food chain, the Inuit depend upon the health of the whole of the Arctic environment. If any of the stages of the food chain beneath them are affected by overuse,

△ An Inuit fishing through the ice.

disease, pollution, or bad weather, their food supply will be affected.

The Inuit understand this. They have a very close spiritual relationship with their environment and a respect for the animals they hunt. They believe that they can kill an

▽ Dog teams are still used in the Arctic.

△ Many Inuit now use snowmobiles on hunting trips.

animal only if the animal agrees to let itself be killed so that the hunter can feed his family. Once an animal is killed it has to be treated with respect by being butchered and eaten in a certain way, otherwise the animal's spirit will bring bad luck on the next hunt. The Inuit see themselves as part of nature, not masters of it.

When the European traders and whalers arrived in the sixteenth century, they had very different ideas about nature. For them the wildlife was there to be exploited. So they hunted to supply markets with blubber and furs, and made a profit by doing so.

However, the Europeans brought new equipment and foods for the Inuit—guns, metal knives and pots, needles, tea, sugar, and much more. To pay for these things many of the Inuit changed their way of life, hunting and trapping animals such as arctic foxes for their fur.

Despite these changes the Inuit still rely on wild animals for most of their food. Their culture is still a hunting culture. Most of the Inuit now live in permanent settlements, which have schools and nursing centers. The hunters have farther to travel to their hunting grounds, and they use motorized snowmobiles and boats with outboard engines to reach them. The money from the sale of seal skins, and polar bear and arctic fox pelts helps to pay for the costs of modern equipment and fuel.

Today the Inuit are at a crossroads. They are learning to deal more effectively with national governments by organizing themselves into village and regional co-operatives and forming political pressure groups. More and more they are being given control over the land and the wildlife on which they depend, and they are voicing their concern at the possible harm that mining and oil drilling are having on wildlife habitats and on their way of life.

Giants of the oceans

The warm-blooded animals that are best adapted for life in the sea have the longest line of marine ancestors. Fossils belonging to early whales go back 60 million years, a long time in the history of mammals. Seals are much younger; their ancestors can be traced back about 15 million years, while it may only be in the last 100,000 years that the polar bear has evolved from its cave bear ancestor, which roamed the European tundras during the last ice age.

Baleen whales

There are two major types of whales. Toothed whales such as dolphins and killer whales hunt animals such as fish and squid. Baleen whales have no teeth. Instead they have long, bony plates in the mouth that are known as baleen, which sieve food from the water. Their main food is animal plankton, which they collect by swimming along with their mouths open. When they close their mouths the water inside is squeezed out through the baleen, and the plankton is trapped on the plates.

The plankton is plentiful only in the spring and summer because the sunlight is too weak in winter for the plant plankton to grow, and the plant plankton is the food for the animal plankton. Baleen whales, therefore, feed only during the summer. In the winter they migrate to subtropical and tropical waters, where they breed and the females give birth to their young. During the winter they have to live off their reserves of blubber, which they accumulated during the summer.

▽ Baleen whales such as the humpback feed on krill and other shrimplike creatures in the plankton.

GREENLAN

△ Commercial whale hunting in the Arctic began nearly 400 years ago (above). Today, most whale hunting is banned and whaling stations (right) are deserted.

Hunting for money

Baleen whales such as blue and fin whales were hunted until they were so few that it was not worth the effort to find them. Today, most countries have passed laws to protect whales, but it may take 100 years for the larger species, the blue and fin whales, to recover their numbers, if they ever do.

The United States was the first country to ban the import of products from whales. However, it has continued to allow the Inuit communities along the Alaskan coast to kill about 41 bowhead whales a year. The Inuit communities of Point Hope and Point Barrow on the northwestern Alaskan coast (see map on page 6) hunt this species. The population of bowhead whales in the western Arctic region is now down to about

7,800 animals, from 20,000 or more in the mid 1800s. However, limited hunting should not threaten this species.

The Inuit communities of this western part of Alaska have for centuries relied upon the annual spring whale hunt to provide much of their food. Whale skin, called muktuk, is considered a delicacy and is an important reason for hunting. It is very high in vitamin C and a very valuable source in a climate where it is not possible to grow vegetables. It is not the fault of the Inuit that the whales have been driven so close to extinction. If they are kept from hunting whales they will also lose an important part of their culture, with its rituals and hunting traditions that are so important to village life.

More mammals

Seals are not as completely adapted for life in the sea as whales are. They have to leave the sea to breed and give birth to their young. The limbs that allow them to move around out of the water make them less streamlined than whales but, like whales, they keep warm by having a thick layer of blubber beneath the skin. They also have a rounded shape and some species grow to a very large size, two features that help seals to save body heat.

Seals do have one advantage over whales in ice-covered seas. Seals are able to haul themselves out of the water onto ice floes, and some species are able to make a breathing hole in the ice and to keep it open through the winter. This allows some seals to live beneath the sea ice even in areas where the ice is a permanent feature, as it is in some areas of Antarctica.

Just as there is more than one major type of whale there is more than one group of seals. There are seals with external (outside) ears (eared seals), and seals with no external ear (called earless seals, although they do have internal ears). Walruses are different enough from other seals for zoologists to put them into a group of their own.

Fur seals

Fur seals and sea lions are eared seals. They have a dense coat of hair, and limbs that are better developed than those of other seals, so they are able to move reasonably well when they are ashore. The earless seals are sometimes called true seals. They have a much thicker layer of blubber than eared seals, which is an advantage in the cold polar waters, but they are clumsier than eared seals when they are ashore or on ice floes.

Back from the brink

Fur seals were once ruthlessly hunted for their dense furs and were easily killed by hunters on their breeding grounds. Overhunting brought the seals close to extinction. The population of the northern species fell from about four million to 134,000 in only 40 years, at the end of the nineteenth century.

Fur seals are no longer hunted in the Antarctic, where there are now at least one million animals. There are probably more fur seals now than there were before the sealers arrived. They have probably increased so much because the overhunting of baleen whales has meant there is more krill for the seals to eat.

◁ Walruses use their tusks to dig up shellfish from the sea bed. Local people carve souvenirs (above) from the ivory tusks.

▷ The northern fur seal was once widely hunted for its fur and nearly became extinct. Today hunting is strictly controlled, and the seal populations have increased.

However, the large populations of fur seals are now damaging the vegetation on their breeding beaches. As the seals move up and down the shore, they rub away the mosses that are helping to hold down the stones on the beaches. The waves then wash over the loose stones and drag them away. Who would have thought that catching whales out in the open ocean, far from land, could lead to beach erosion?

The earless seals

There are five species of earless seals in the Antarctic and 10 in the Arctic. The largest species is the elephant seal, with the bulls (males) weighing over 6,600 lb when fully grown. Like the fur seal, it is not a species that belongs to the pack ice but lives around the sub-Antarctic islands, such as South Georgia, where it breeds in large colonies. Male elephant seals defend their territory by roaring at any rivals that come too close. They increase the volume by inflating their huge noses. If that doesn't deter the rival, then a fight may follow.

Elephant seals are clumsy and ungainly ashore, but they are expert hunters in the sea. The water supports their great weight as they search for their favorite food—squid.

The other species of Antarctic seals are the Weddell, Ross, leopard, and crab-eater seals, which all live amid the

sea ice. The Weddell seal is the truest ice species in the Antarctic, for it lives beneath the landfast ice that is attached to the edge of the Antarctic continent. It keeps a breathing hole open by chipping the ice away with its teeth, sometimes until its gums bleed and stain the snow red.

The Ross seal lives out on the thick pack ice far from shore, and very little is known about it. The leopard seal is a lone hunter, mostly of crab-eater seals and penguins. It has a long neck, which it uses to kill its prey by shaking it from side to side. Leopard seals are able to shake penguins out of their skins, which makes eating them much easier than eating a body covered with feathers.

The most abundant seal in the world is the crab-eater seal (which does not eat crabs!). The population is somewhere around 15 million. Like fur seals, the crab-eater feeds on krill and may have benefited by the reduction in baleen whales as well.

Although 10 species of seals live in various parts of the Arctic Ocean, only two, the ringed seal and the bearded seal, are true polar species.

The type of ice is important to the ringed seal. It breeds out on the stable first-year ice, for this is where ice hummocks and pressure ridges allow snow to accumulate. It is in the drifts beside the hummocks that the females make their birth lairs in which the young are born.

△ Male elephant seals roar and fight with each other to keep rivals away.

24

△ The ringed seal is the smallest but the most common of the Arctic seals.

The ringed seal feeds on a wide variety of animals, including arctic mussels and polar cod. It likes the open water channels and polynyas that develop where the pack ice splits apart, for here it can reach the surface for air and haul itself out on to the ice to rest.

Taking aim
The ringed seal is the most important animal for the Inuit. The blubber is rich in energy and the meat provides protein, minerals and vitamins. Even today, with most villages having stores and supermarkets, the ringed seal provides the Inuit with nearly three quarters of their food. Seal skin is used to make waterproof mukluks (boots) and parkas (coats with a hood), but today most of the skins are sold, and the money is used to buy guns, ammunition, and other goods.

The Inuit hunt the ringed seal in three kinds of habitat, and each one requires a different method. On the landfast ice attached to the shore the hunters try to spot seals that have hauled up on the ice. Once one is spotted the hunter stalks to within 500 feet before shooting. In the winter and spring the hunting is along the edges of the ice floes. Once a seal's head is spotted the marksman has only a few seconds to make the shot. The seal is retrieved in a small canvas-covered plywood skiff. In the summer and autumn, before freeze-up, seals are hunted from canoes in the open water.

So far the number of seals killed by Inuit hunters is only a small part of the total population – between 50,000 and 70,000 a year. In 1981 the Inuit population in the Canadian Arctic was 13,000. This may rise to 37,500 by the year 2001, so unless the life-style of the Inuit changes considerably the demand for seal meat will increase over the next decade.

▷ The Inuit sometimes use seal oil for heating, lighting, and cooking.

Summer visitors

There are advantages for many species of animals in being only summer visitors to the polar regions. In both the polar oceans and on the tundra, plant and invertebrate food is plentiful only in the summer. During the rest of the year, when the weather conditions are at their worst, there is little to eat.

Another advantage of moving into the polar regions is that migrating animals leave behind the predators that threaten them in their winter quarters. Since very little wildlife spends the winter in the polar regions, there is very little food for predators, so the number of predators is low. The Arctic tundra, in particular, is a favored habitat for caribou, migratory waterfowl, and waders in which to raise their young. Some predators, such as the arctic skua, do migrate with the

birds they prey on, but most predators have territories that they do not or cannot leave.

However, in regions where human populations are large, migrating animals can be faced with damage to either their summer or winter habitats or both, and they may be hunted by humans all along their migration routes. Fortunately there are also plenty of cases where the needs of migrating animals have brought people from different countries together to safeguard the animals and their habitat.

Wanderers of the north

If one animal typifies the Arctic tundra it must be the caribou (in North America) and the closely related reindeer (in Europe and Asia). Most caribou spend the winter in the

▷ Most caribou spend the winter in the shelter of the northern forests. They move out onto the tundra in the spring. The herds may have to cross water (above) on their long migration journeys.

△ In the forest, the wolf is the main enemy of the caribou.

shelter of the northern forests, where they rely upon the lichens. In spring the caribou migrate out onto the tundra, allowing the calves to be born in areas where there are few wolves, the main predators of the calves.

There are several caribou herds spread across northern Canada and Alaska. Each one has more or less its own area of forest and tundra in which it spends most of its time. However, caribou herds are famous for unpredictable crashes in population and changes in migration routes, which in the past left those Inuit that relied upon caribou meat starving. There could be several reasons why caribou numbers may drop very rapidly at times. The herds may overgraze their summer pastures, forest fires may wipe out lichens, abnormal weather conditions may cover their food plants in spring with a layer of ice, and sometimes too many animals are killed by hunters.

To the Inuit, the caribou is second only to the ringed seal as a food animal. On Banks Island (see map on page 6) a hunter kills an average of 16 caribou a year, which is enough for about one quarter of a family's food needs. Lapps and many of the Arctic tribes in the Soviet Union also rely upon the reindeer to provide a living, but instead of hunting wild animals they have herds of semi-domesticated animals.

In the 1980s the numbers of one of the largest herds of wild caribou in Canada, the Beverly-Kaminuriak herd, which spends the summer on the tundra of the Barren Grounds, seemed to be dropping alarmingly. The Canadian Government decided to involve the local Inuit in finding a solution on how to manage the Beverly herd, as they were the people with most to lose if it decreased in size. The local hunters did not think the herd was decreasing, and they were later proved to be right, but they agreed to the setting up of a caribou management board which included members of the local villages as well as government officials.

The management board in effect gives the local Inuit a lot of control over how the caribou herd is used, how many animals are killed each year, by whom and at what time of year. When people have control over the resources that are important to them they are much more likely to look after them properly, because they have everything to gain by doing so.

However, the Beverly caribou herd is most at risk not on the tundra, but in the coniferous forest to the south, where the animals spend the winter. In particular, the lichens which the caribou need in winter are plentiful only in areas that have remained unburned for many years. Fires are common in the coniferous forests. Some start naturally by lightning or by accident, while some may be started deliberately to improve the growth of shrubs for moose, the most valuable game animal for the forest Indians.

The management board has made recommendations on how to safeguard the forest habitat, but the Inuit have no real control over what happens there. The Beverly-Kaminuriak caribou herd illustrates the problems in managing animals that live in different regions at different times of year, with each region supporting people with different needs.

On the wing

In some ways the problems in looking after the populations of the migrating birds such as geese are much greater than those in managing a large mammal like the caribou. Over the course of a single year birds may spend time in three or more countries, and looking after their habitats and regulating hunting can be quite a problem.

The sight and sound of a large skein of geese coming out of the northern sky in autumn is one that has filled many a naturalist's heart with a sense of wonder. What wild lands have they come from? What stories would they tell if they could speak to humans? Modern communications and radio-tracking, which allow scientists to visit the geese and to follow their every move, has

taken away some of the magic, perhaps, but there is still plenty left to wonder at.

The Arctic is an important breeding area for many species of northern hemisphere geese. Geese are one of the three families of waterfowl, the others being ducks and swans. The northern hemisphere geese can be divided into two major groups—gray geese and black geese. The gray geese include the graylag, pinkfoot, whitefront, and snow goose. Canada geese, barnacle, and brant are black geese.

By moving north into the Arctic for the summer, geese can take advantage of the summer burst in the growth of plants, and insects and other invertebrates, and escape many of their predators while they are raising their goslings.

△ Canada goose

▷ The moose feeds on willow, and shrubs that flourish after forest fires.

▽ Graylag goose

However, nesting in the Arctic has its dangers. Because the summer is short, only about 75 to 80 days, there is barely enough time for geese to lay their eggs, hatch them and raise their young before winter sets in. The danger for geese is that a late spring will not give them enough time, and then breeding can fail. The farther north the geese breed, the greater the danger that this will happen. Many geese, especially brant geese, which breed in the high Arctic, start nesting before the winter snows have melted, so that the goslings hatch just at the time plants begin to grow. However, if the snows melt late many of the goslings will starve to death.

In the wintering grounds to the south there have been many changes since the end of the last ice age. First, there was open ground available as the ice sheets melted, but soon trees covered the land with forests, and geese were forced out to marshes and coastal estuaries. No sooner had the forest spread than, in Europe at least, along came farmers who cut and burned them down to create meadows and fields. Geese, which are grazing animals, must have benefited by the change back to open habitats.

On the other hand, the salt marshes and coasts, where many geese spend the winter, are often prime sites for farms, ports, power stations, oil refineries, and pleasure marinas. Goose hunting is also a popular activity, and each winter many are shot.

Over the years many marshes have been drained and plowed to grow crops, but with the overproduction of cereals in Europe and North America, farmers are now being paid a cash grant by some governments if they keep their grasslands for the conservation of wildlife. Geese are also very adaptable and have learned to feed on new foods, such as potatoes, wheat, and rice. These crops provide geese with better nourishment than their natural winter foods, so the geese are in much better condition when they leave for their Arctic breeding grounds in the spring.

△ Geese feed on the roots and shoots of cotton grass.

The lesser snow goose

The lesser snow goose is a major Arctic species with a breeding range from eastern Siberia to Baffin Island in Canada. There are over 12 major breeding colonies, and the snow goose population in the eastern Canadian Arctic is almost a million birds.

Large numbers of snow geese

Snow goose

spend the winter on the marshes along the coast of the Gulf of Mexico, and this is where much of the sport hunting takes place. Recently, the geese have learned to use the rice fields inland, and winter refuges have been established where rice is grown specially for the geese. The winter habitat of geese is more and more a farmed one, and it is only in the Arctic breeding habitats that they are birds of truly wild ecosystems.

Indians and Inuit kill large numbers of snow geese, as well as taking many eggs. Snow geese are also popular prey for sport hunters. Many sport hunters want the spring hunting of geese completely banned to allow as many geese to nest and raise young as possible. But for indigenous people in the Arctic fresh goose meat in the spring is a welcome change of diet at the end of a long cold winter, and they look forward to a supply of fresh goose eggs. The conservation of waterfowl and the regulation of shooting is very advanced in North America and there are management agreements with the Inuit on how many geese they will kill each spring and how many eggs they will take. The numbers depend on how successful the previous breeding season has been and how well the birds have survived the winter.

The behavior of sport hunters has also been studied and it has been found that fewer birds are wounded and fewer birds shot at if hunters are strictly limited in the number of shotgun cartridges they are allowed to use and the number of geese they can shoot in a day. The future for North American geese seems, on the whole, bright despite the problems in managing species that migrate the length of North America.

Wading birds

Waders are long-legged and mostly long-billed birds of marshes and mudflats. Many of them live in large flocks, particularly in winter when they move south from the Arctic to wintering grounds as far away as Africa and Australia. There are altogether nine major groups or families of wading birds, including plovers, sandpipers, and phalaropes. The Arctic tundra bogs and marshes that have developed on the flat ground above the permafrost are the major breeding habitat for most wading birds.

Among the waders that breed in the Arctic is the red-necked phalarope, which spends the winter out at sea but nests on the tundra ponds and slow-moving watercourses. It has a special way of catching its food, usually insects such as mosquito larvae. It whirls around in a circle, creating a vortex in the water beneath it which sucks up the small animals to the surface.

Like the migrating waterfowl, the waders have to arrive in the Arctic in good condition because spring is often not under way for several days after their arrival. Sometimes, of course, spring is late and the birds

Red-necked phalarope

may have to lay their eggs while there is still a lot of snow and very little to eat. It is very important for these birds that they have good staging areas, particularly estuaries, along their migration routes, where they can refuel with supplies of rich food. Pollution, and the draining of coastal mudflats for farming and industry are major dangers to wading bird populations.

Great bear and little fox

The polar bear

The polar bear is about twice the size of a lion or tiger. Its main food is seals, particularly the ringed seal. The polar bear is an animal of the pack ice. Without the sea ice, it would never be able to take advantage of the food available in the polar seas. The polar bear is a good swimmer, and young ones seem to enjoy playing together in the water. Adult bears have sometimes been seen swimming many miles from the nearest shore or ice floe.

Out on the pack ice most bears are solitary creatures, but they do not appear to be unsociable animals. They probably spend most of their time alone simply because they have to get close enough to seals to kill them. When they come ashore as the outer pack ice breaks up in the summer they seem to enjoy the company of other bears and have been seen playing together.

The polar bear is very well adapted for life on the pack ice. It has thick fur and a thick layer of fat beneath the skin, which provide excellent insulation against the cold. The fat is particularly important when the bear is swimming, because its fur does not hold a layer of warm air when it gets wet. The hairs are also hollow, so that ultraviolet rays from the sun can pass through them and be absorbed by the black skin beneath. On land, the white fur is excellent camouflage.

The polar bear has a superb sense of smell, which is a great advantage out on the pack ice in winter. When it is dark or only twilight it is difficult to see the open water pools and channels in the ice from a distance, but these are places where the seals are to be found. Some naturalists think polar bears may be able to smell seals and meat from 12 miles or more away.

△ A polar bear spreads its weight on thin ice as it hunts seals.

▷ Polar bears have better eyesight than most other bears and a sharp sense of smell.

Walking on ice

Polar bears have been recorded within 125 miles of the North Pole, but the central part of the Arctic Basin, with its thick mass of permanent pack ice, supports few seals or other animals. Most bears are found within 125 to 185 miles of the shore. Although polar bears can wander very long distances, especially on drifting ice, they usually stay in a "home" area. Across the Arctic there are about 12 different populations. The world population is about 25,000 and of these, 15,000 animals live in the Canadian Arctic. About 3,000 bears live around Svalbard, and large numbers are thought to live on the edge of the pack ice in the rich waters between Svalbard and northeast Greenland. Occasionally drifting winter pack ice has brought polar bears to the coast of Iceland.

In Canada bears are plentiful along the shores of Hudson Bay, where the melting of the pack ice in the summer forces them ashore until the sea freezes over again in the fall. For most of the summer they have to fast until they are able to return to seal hunting,

△ Polar bears give birth to cubs every two or three years.

although they do eat what they can find, for example dead animals washed up on the tideline, berries and, more recently, leftovers from the rubbish dumps of the town of Churchill.

Family life
The female bears come ashore to give birth. The babies are born in dens made in the steep snowbanks along the slopes of coastal hills and valley sides. The pregnant bears go into their dens in November, and the cubs are born in December. At birth they are blind and weigh under 20 pounds. Both the mother and the cubs remain in the den until March or early April.

There are certain parts of the Arctic favored by bears for dens. In Canada dens are plentiful on the southern side of Banks Island and Victoria Island. In the Soviet Union, Wrangel Island, which is about a week's walk from Alaska for a polar bear, has many dens. (See map on page 6.) Other popular areas are east Greenland and Svalbard.

A female polar bear will breed at about four years of age and give birth every three years. However, the bears living in the Hudson Bay breed more often, about every other year, so presumably the southern bears have an easier life than their northern relatives.

People on the prowl
The Inuit hunt polar bears mainly for their pelts, which sell for high prices in the fur markets of southern Canada. For the Inuit, however, the polar bear also has a spiritual importance. Before the Europeans came to the Arctic the Inuit considered the bear to be in touch with the spirit world. When a bear was killed, its spirit had to be honored by a ceremony lasting several days.

The meat is regarded as a delicacy, although it is usually heavily infested with a parasite called trichinosis, and bear liver is so rich in vitamin A that eating it can cause blindness. Polar bear fur is used to lubricate the sledge runners to make them run more easily over the snow.

Polar bears are normally hunted on the pack ice, and an average trip takes about two weeks. The hunters may travel almost 200 miles. If a dog team is used to pull the sled the dogs can be relied upon to detect the bear's scent and to give chase. In the days before the Inuit had firearms, the kill had to be made with a spear, which required courage, good timing and strength.

Sport hunting for polar bears is allowed in Canada but the hunters have to be guided by the Inuit, and any bear killed counts as part of the quota allowed to each village that is in a bear area. At one time it was legal to hunt polar bears in Alaska by using aircraft to spot them and then landing the hunters on the pack ice. And around Svalbard, shooting of polar bears from ships was allowed. Both these ways of killing bears are no longer legal, and all hunting on Svalbard and in the Soviet Union has now been stopped. People there are only allowed to kill bears in self-defense.

The arctic fox

Like the polar bear, the arctic fox is learning to take advantage of the supplies of food in the polar seas, which are richer than in the tundra. In the winter many arctic foxes rely on the leftovers of the bears' kills. When bears find plenty of their favorite prey, the ringed seal, they eat only the blubber, leaving the rest of the carcass. The arctic fox follows the bears and finds an easy meal.

In summer, the foxes are forced ashore to breed as the pack ice breaks up and melts. The foxes usually make their dens along the coastline, where they raid the nests of sea birds and waterfowl. In the winter, arctic foxes grow a dense white fur, which has been a valuable commodity in southern fur markets. Where there are many arctic foxes, the Inuit put fox trapping high on their list of priorities, since the sale of furs is the best source of income.

Like some other mammals of the North, the Arctic fox has a white coat in the winter (left), which changes in the summer (above).

The hardy ones

Very few species of land animals spend the winter in the polar regions, a sign perhaps that the polar environments are new ones to which few animals have had a chance to adapt fully. The Arctic fares much better than the Antarctic. The milder climate means more food is available for a much wider range of animals. And the fact that it has also been possible for land animals to walk into the Arctic as the climate improved at the end of the last ice age is no doubt also a reason. (The Antarctic continent, by contrast, was isolated from others by ocean.) The animals that spend the winter in the Arctic are the ones that have a long history of living in cold climates. It is possible that more species may be able to adapt to the polar winter in the future. Of the Arctic land mammals only the musk ox, arctic hare, caribou, and wolf are active above the surface in winter, and most of the caribou leave the tundra for the forests to the south. Birds are better equipped to survive extreme cold and icy winds than mammals, because down is a much better insulator than hair. Ptarmigans, snowy owls, ravens, arctic redpolls, and snow buntings are all able to stay active through the winter.

△ The snow bunting is a common tundra bird. It feeds mainly on grass seeds.

▷ The Arctic hare has small ears to prevent heat loss.

Ice age ancestors

The musk ox, the largest land animal in the Arctic, has a long history of living in cold, dry glacial climates. Fossils have been found in eastern England and Europe dating well back into the Ice Age.

The adults are about the size of a cow and have a humped profile very similar to a bison's, but they are also related to goats. In winter the musk oxen feed on the ridges and hills which, although very cold, are kept free of snow by the strong winds. They have become superbly adapted for life on the Arctic tundra.

Large animals lose less heat for their size than smaller ones, so their large size is a help. They also have short, stumpy legs, so there is less area of skin through which to lose valuable body heat. But it is their coat that really keeps them warm. It is made of two layers, each with a different kind of hair. The outer layer consists of long guard hairs,

▷ The musk ox, the largest land mammal in the Arctic, lives on the open plains and hills.

which trail almost to the ground. This layer is almost airtight and protects the inner coat, which is made of a dense layer of very fine wool, which the Inuit call qiviut. It is so fine that one ounce provides enough yarn to make a skirt. Since the 1960s there have been experimental efforts to domesticate the musk ox as a luxury wool-producing animal for the Inuit to farm.

Musk oxen have a very efficient digestive system and body chemistry that are able to make the most of small amounts of often poor food in the winter. In the summer some of the arctic plants, such as willows, sedges, and cotton grass, provide very nutritious food, and the animals are able to accumulate large reserves of fat to help them get through the winter months.

On the tundra the musk ox herds are easily found by the few packs of wolves that manage to survive the long winters until the musk ox calves are born in the spring. However, wolves do not find the musk oxen easy to kill. When the herds are attacked, the adult animals form a circle with the calves

inside it. With their curved, sweeping horns the musk oxen are able to repel most wolf attacks.

However, this method of defense is useless against men with firearms. Musk oxen were still common in the 1850s, but by the end of the nineteenth century few were left. Canada gave its remaining animals full legal protection in 1917 and since then their numbers have been steadily increasing. Animals are also being reintroduced to areas where they had disappeared, such as northern Alaska. The musk ox today is doing well. And because it does not migrate, there are fewer problems in looking after the herds than there are with caribou (see page 26).

Small mammals

At the other end of the size scale are the voles, lemmings, and ground squirrels, which are too small to remain active above ground in winter. They would lose too much body heat. These animals have a system of tunnels and chambers where the ground is dry. The lemmings actually remain active

▷ The ground squirrel survives the Arctic winter by hibernating in a burrow.

△ The snowy owl feeds on lemmings and other rodents and on rabbits.

beneath the snow in winter but the ground squirrels hibernate from early winter through to the spring.

After one or two good summers there is plenty of food for these plant-eating mammals, and they have a remarkable ability to breed when times are good. Two adult lemmings can produce 40 young over two breeding seasons, so their numbers can increase rapidly when there is plenty of food.

The predators, such as snowy owls, arctic foxes, and wolves then have more food than they can eat and so they too raise more young. But the good times do not last forever in the Arctic, and the time comes when the small mammals are eating the plants faster than they grow. When that happens, they die by the thousands, of disease and starvation, and soon the predators are starving too. Only the fittest ones will survive until better times return. Great fluctuations in the size of animal populations are a feature of polar ecosystems. They are the result of

an unpredictable climate. If the spring is cold and the snow is late in melting, many animals are unable to raise their young. Their numbers decrease and so do the predators that depend upon them for food.

▽ The lynx preys on Arctic hares, ground squirrels, lemmings, and other small mammals.

Petrels and penguins

The polar seas are rich feeding grounds for sea birds. Of all the species of sea birds that spend at least part of the year in the polar regions, none of them is better adapted for using the rich supplies of food available in the polar sea than petrels and penguins of Antarctica. They are the most numerous birds around the Antarctic continent.

Petrels are long-winged birds, about the size of a pigeon, that skim the surface of the sea for food, usually plankton. In Antarctica there are two species that are true birds of the sea ice—the snow petrel and the antarctic petrel. The boundary of their world is the ring of ice floes that pile up in summer around the Antarctic continent (see page 10). They are also the only bird known to breed deep in the interior of the Antarctic continent, where they lay their eggs on crevices and exposed rock ledges.

The snow petrel and antarctic petrel roam over the pack ice, hunting the krill, and they often roost on icebergs, swarming around much as city pigeons do around tall buildings. Unlike the other petrels, they have wings adapted for flight over flat ice surfaces in breezes, rather than for flight in high winds deflected from waves.

Dressed for survival

Penguins are adapted for the polar seas in a very different way from the petrels. Instead of skimming over the surface of the sea, penguins swim beneath it in search of food. Their bullet-shaped bodies are streamlined in much the same way as those of whales and seals. Like seals, they pay a price for this streamlined shape when they leave the water to rest and breed. Their legs are short and set well back on long bodies, which makes them walk with a waddle. Their wings are used as paddles under water and have lost the power of flight.

Like all birds, penguins reproduce by laying eggs, so, however well-adapted they are for swimming and hunting in the sea, they are forced to leave the water to breed. Incredible as it may seem, the emperor penguin breeds in the middle of the coldest season in the coldest region of the earth. All the other six species breed in the summer; so what is the advantage of winter breeding for the emperor? Since it is the largest species, its chicks take the longest time to grow and mature. If they were hatched in early summer they would reach the age to be independent just as winter was coming on. Midwinter breeding ensures that the chicks mature just as the Antarctic summer begins.

There are 30 breeding colonies, and most of them are on the landfast ice, which is stable from early winter until the spring break-up. The female emperor lays a single egg in May or early June (the beginning of winter in Antarctica), which is incubated by the male. He balances the egg on his feet and covers it with a special fold of skin. Once the male is looking after the egg the female returns to the sea, sometimes traveling 60 miles or more across the ice to reach open water. The females return in July, midwinter in Antarctica. The males, meanwhile, incubate the eggs at a time of year when the average temperature is about −4°F, and during this time they are not able to eat. They have to rely on their supplies of body fat to provide the energy and water they need. In the three months of winter fasting they lose 40 percent of their body weight. The birds huddle together to save body heat and thus make their reserves of fat last longer. Their large size also helps in reducing the loss of heat. They are less affected by the blizzards that rage across the landfast ice for days at a time than smaller penguins would be.

Once the chicks hatch in July they are fed and looked after by the female, while the male returns to the sea to feed. As the chicks get older they group together in crèches while both parents search for food. The chicks molt in December or January, about the time that the landfast ice starts to break up. The young birds finish growing on an ice floe among the pack ice.

Pesticide pollution
Penguins have never been hunted to any real extent by humans but they have not entirely escaped the effects of man. Like that of the ringed seal in the Arctic, the penguins' flesh now contains small amounts of pesticides and heavy metals that pollute the sea. Also, because 99 percent of the Antarctic continent is covered with permanent ice, penguins and scientists are sometimes in competition for the most suitable ice-free sites. Most of the penguin species, other than the emperor, breed on the land close to the sea. The competition for available space between wildlife and man is of great concern to conservationists, and the problem could get worse if the exploration for minerals and oil were to increase.

The emperor is the largest penguin of all. The female lays a single egg, which the male incubates under a special fold of skin (left). When the chicks hatch they stay in groups (above).

Polar prospects for the future

The threats to the polar regions have come not from the indigenous people but from outside. There are three types of threat. One is overhunting (including overfishing) of wildlife. The second is damage to the polar habitats caused by the drilling and mining for oil, gas, and minerals. The third type of threat is the effect of pollution.

Pollution is the most difficult problem to solve because it comes from the way almost everyone lives. Most of us eat food that has been grown by using pesticides, buy goods that produce heavy metals in the manufacturing processes, and use cars that push carbon dioxide into the air. In time, these substances find their way into the polar ecosystems. So far, the amounts of pesticides and heavy metals are small, but the fact that they have been found in Antarctic penguins and Arctic ringed seals shows that they eventually spread to the most isolated parts of the planet.

No one can yet be sure what effects the rise in carbon dioxide levels will have on the climate. No doubt some species of wildlife will gain and others lose if the climate becomes warmer. Radioactive fallout, on the other hand, offers no advantages. Grazing animals, such as reindeer, are particularly affected by nuclear fallout in the Arctic because they eat lichens, which absorb radioactive substances very easily. The Chernobyl nuclear power plant accident in the Soviet Union has had disastrous effects on the Lapplanders' reindeer industry. The animals have levels of radiation above government safety levels and cannot be used as food.

Overhunting is less of a problem than it used to be. The countries that have Arctic tundra have each taken steps to control hunting in their territories. More and more local communities are being given the right to control the way that wildlife and the wildlife habitats are managed.

It is difficult to protect animals that migrate and use habitats in more than one country, but international agreements have made the task easier. In 1916 the United States and Canada signed a treaty to regulate the hunting of migrating waterfowl such as ducks and geese. In the 1980s many nations signed the Ramsar Treaty, by which they agreed to protect the wetland habitats that are so vital for water birds. International agreements also exist to safeguard the future of polar bears, which do sometimes wander between Arctic countries.

It is much more difficult to protect animals that live in the oceans, because the oceans belong to no one and, therefore, no one has control over what other nations do, unless countries agree to work together.

Several countries have had claims to parts of Antarctica but these claims were not recognized by everyone. This could have led to major international disputes, with terrible effects on a natural and virtually untouched part of the world. Fortunately, good sense won the day and all claims have been suspended indefinitely. This act of good faith was followed in 1959 by an Antarctic Treaty designed to protect the continent and allow scientific work to continue.

The treaty has, over the years, been widened to include more aspects of the Antarctic environment. Thirty-nine countries have now signed it. At first the treaty only concentrated on the continent and its fringes, but almost all the animals of Antarctica rely upon the sea for their food. It is now widely accepted that we also need to look after the ocean around the continent.

Safety for seals

In 1972 an agreement was reached on the conservation of Antarctic seals. Fur seals, elephant seals, and Ross seals were totally protected, and catch limits were set for the other seals. However, there is no

△ Penguins and scientists sometimes have to share the same space.

commercial hunting of pack ice seals in Antarctica.

The Convention on Antarctic Seals was followed in 1980 by a major step forward. Agreement was reached to protect more than seals in a new convention called the Convention on the Conservation of Antarctic Marine Living Resources (CCAMLR). Its aim is to protect the Antarctic ecosystem and to carry out research to learn how to look after it. This means understanding the ocean habitat and the plants and animals that live in it. The idea is to use this knowledge to build a model of the Antarctic. Such a model will help scientists to predict the effects of krill-catching, fishing, and pollution on the ecosystem.

Looking for oil

In 1988 another convention was agreed to by several nations to regulate the exploration for and exploitation of oil, gas, and minerals, to limit environmental damage. However, some countries have refused to sign the convention and Antarctica has become the center of a debate on whether to completely ban mining or not.

At the present time it is not practical to drill for oil or mine minerals in the Antarctic. On land the ice sheet is just too thick, and out at sea there are too many problems with operating rigs. The waters are deep, and the seas are very stormy and full of icebergs.

However, this does not mean that these problems will not be solved in the future. Some countries, supported by Greenpeace and the World Wide Fund for Nature, believe the only way to preserve Antarctica as the last great wilderness is to ban mining for all time and turn Antarctica into a "World Park" to be run by the United Nations. The danger in that idea is that it could take years to reach an international agreement to bring it about.

In the less hostile Arctic many of the problems that made mining and oil drilling almost unthinkable 20 years ago have been overcome. Large-scale projects can cause damage, especially if mistakes are made in operating equipment, causing oil spills for example, but the record of the oil companies in extracting oil from the Prudhoe Bay field in arctic Alaska has been good. Birds nest close to the work sites, and caribou often wander between the oil derricks, apparently unconcerned.

Oil companies in Alaska are now exploring for oil off the northern coast. The local Inuit are worried about the effects of oil extraction on the migration of whales. They are concerned that vibrations in the water from the rigs may upset the animals. They are also worried about the effect of oil spills on marine life.

Oil companies also want to explore for oil in the Arctic Wildlife Range to the east of Prudhoe Bay. This area is the summer calving ground for the large Porcupine caribou herd. Development here worries the Indians who hunt these caribou in their winter forests.

▽ Many organizations are fighting to protect the beauty of the Antarctic.

Village life
The greatest effect of big mining and oil projects has been on the local Inuit villages that suddenly find dozens or hundreds of people from the south, who have little understanding of the Arctic, or their way of life, in their midst. However, the Inuit are better organized than they were 20 years ago. In Alaska, native communities have been allowed to claim large areas of land, and this is also happening in Canada. Oil and mining companies have to reach agreements and pay royalties to the local communities if they want to exploit the resources on land belonging to indigenous people. The conditions put on mining and oil companies are generally quite tough.

It is our demands for oil and minerals, and the pollution we all produce that are the modern threats to life in the polar regions. Strange as it may seem, we could be doing more harm to the Arctic by driving our cars than by buying a seal or polar bear skin from the Inuit hunters who kill animals to put food on their families' tables.

Index